World Languages

Colors in
Spanish

Daniel Nunn

Chicago, Illinois

www.capstonepub.com
Visit our website to find out more information about Heinemann-Raintree books.

To order:
☎ Phone 800-747-4992
💻 Visit www.capstonepub.com to browse our catalog and order online.

Edited by Rebecca Rissman, Dan Nunn, and Sian Smith
Designed by Joanna Hinton-Malivoire
Picture research by Elizabeth Alexander
Production by Alison Parsons
Originated by Capstone Global Library Ltd
Printed and bound in the United States of America in North Mankato, MN. 032013 007231RP

16 15 14 13
10 9 8 7 6 5 4 3 2

Library of Congress Cataloging-in-Publication Data
Nunn, Daniel.
  Colors in Spanish : los colores / Daniel Nunn.
    p. cm.—(World languages - Colors)
  Includes bibliographical references and index.
  ISBN 978-1-4329-6652-2—ISBN 978-1-4329-6659-1 (pbk.)
1. Spanish language—Textbooks for foreign speakers—EnglishvJuvenile literature. 2. Colors—Juvenile literature. I. Title.
  PC4129.E5N86 2013
  468.2'421—dc23   2011046562

Acknowledgments
We would like to thank Shutterstock for permission to reproduce photographs: pp.4 (© Phiseksit), 5 (© Stephen Aaron Rees), 6 (© Tischenko Irina), 7 (© Tony Magdaraog), 8 (© szefei), 9 (© Picsfive), 10 (© Eric Isselée), 11 (© Yasonya), 12 (© Nadezhda Bolotina), 13 (© Maryna Gviazdovska), 14 (© Erik Lam), 15 (© Eric Isselée), 16 (© Ruth Black), 17 (© blueskies9), 18 (© Alexander Dashewsky), 19 (© Michele Perbellini), 20 (© Eric Isselée), 21 (© Roman Rvachov).

Cover photographs reproduced with permission of Shutterstock: dog (© Erik Lam), strawberry (© Stephen Aaron Rees), fish (© Tischenko Irina). Back cover photograph of a cup reproduced with permission of Shutterstock (© Maryna Gviazdovska).

We would like to thank Rebeca Otazua Bideganeta and Silvia Vázquez-Fernández for their invaluable assistance in the preparation of this book.

Every effort has been made to contact copyright holders of material reproduced in this book. Any omissions will be rectified in subsequent printings if notice is given to the publisher.

Contents

Rojo

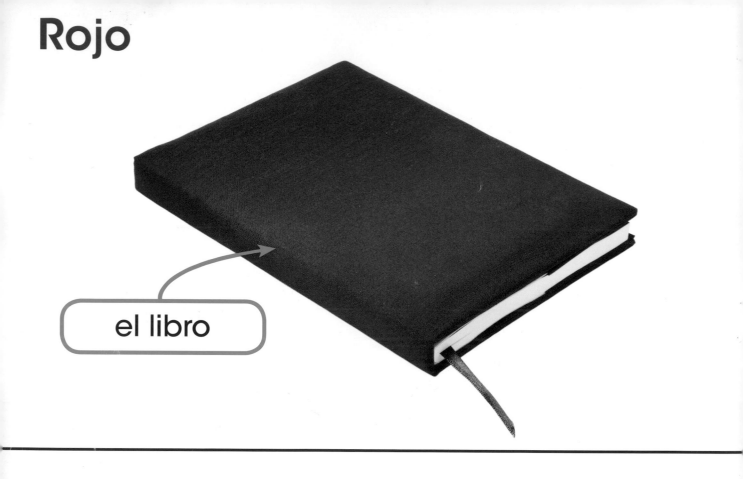

el libro

El libro es rojo.

la fresa

La fresa es roja.

Naranja

el pez

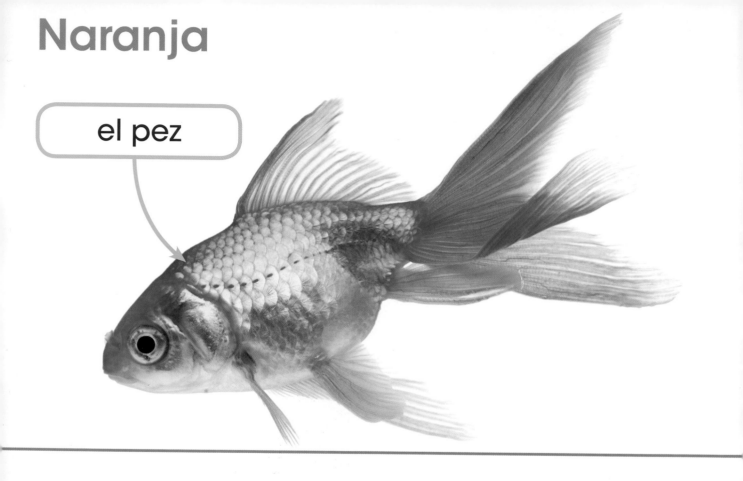

El pez es naranja.

la zanahoria

La zanahoria es naranja.

Amarillo

la flor

La flor es amarilla.

el plátano

El plátano es amarillo.

Verde

el pájaro

El pájaro es verde.

la manzana

La manzana es verde.

Azul

la camiseta

La camiseta es azul.

la taza

La taza es azul.

Marrón

el perro

El perro es marrón.

la vaca

La vaca es marrón.

Rosa

la torta

La torta es rosa.

el sombrero

El sombrero es rosa.

Blanca

la leche

La leche es blanca.

la nieve

La nieve es blanca.

Negro

El gato es **negro**.

el paraguas

El paraguas es **negro**.

Dictionary

Spanish Word	How To Say It	English Word
amarilla	a-ma-ree-ya	yellow (feminine)
amarillo	a-ma-ree-yo	yellow (masculine)
azul	a-thul	blue
blanca	blan-ca	white
camiseta	cam-ee-say-ta	T-shirt
el	el	the (masculine)
es	es	is
flor	floor	flower
fresa	fray-sa	strawberry
gato	gat-o	cat
la	la	the (feminine)
leche	letch-ay	milk
libro	lee-bro	book
manzana	man-than-na	apple
marrón	mar-ron	brown
naranja	na-ran-ha	orange

Spanish Word	How To Say It	English Word
negro	neh-gro	black
nieve	nee-eh-beh	snow
pájaro	paa-ha-ro	bird
paraguas	pah-raa-gwas	umbrella
perro	per-ro	dog
pez	peth	fish
plátano	plaa-tan-o	banana
roja	ro-ha	red (feminine)
rojo	ro-ho	red (masculine)
rosa	ro-sa	pink
sombrero	som-brer-o	hat
taza	ta-tha	cup
torta	tort-ta	cake
vaca	bac-a	cow
verde	bear-day	green
zanahoria	than-a-horia	carrot

See words in the "How To Say It" columns for a rough guide to pronunciations.

Index

Notes for Parents and Teachers

In Spanish, nouns are either masculine or feminine. The word for "the" changes accordingly—either el (masculine) or la (feminine). Sometimes adjectives have different spellings too, depending on whether the noun is masculine or feminine. This is why some of the colors have more than one spelling.